an
Orphan
No More

Accepting My New Identity

Rocky Fleming

Prayer Cottage Publications

BELLA VISTA, ARKANSAS

"So then you are no longer strangers and aliens, but you are fellow citizens with the saints and members of the household of God."—Ephesians 2:19 ESV

Prayer Cottage Publications – Rogers, AR

INFLUENCERS
— GLOBAL MINISTRIES —

Mission: To encourage and influence individuals toward an abiding relationship with Jesus Christ, through a journey to spiritual intimacy.

Vision: To transform lives through The Journey, enabling them to be a positive influence to their world around them.

Contents

Dear Reader,

*The book you are about to read is an allegory of truth.
The story and characters are fictional, and yet they are
as real as your next-door neighbor, or even your own
self. It is as real as the life stories of those who have
walked this earth. It is as real as my own life story and
those of loved ones and friends and people who have
influenced me. It is from these sources that I find real
life examples to use as fictional characters. These things
form my thoughts and creative illustrations to use in my
books. I could not write my books with only the theory
of a life lived in close proximity with Christ. I must write
them with the truths that I have personally discovered
in my walk with Him. That is how I can say that this is
a fictional story based on real people and real truths. I
have seen these truths.*

*My books are written to awaken these truths in you and
to point my readers to the truth of what Jesus offers His
family. Too often we do not look deeper into our relationship with Him. Too often we do not fully accept the
freedom and transformation that He gives to a man or*

woman, for we do not know there is more beyond our initial point of salvation. But there is so much more, and when we discover it we enter into an intimate relationship with God that we never thought possible. I ask you to enter in as you read this book. There is a feast to be found. I pray that you and your HEAVENLY DADDY will draw close, and His Spirit will tell you what might be missing and how it can be found.

I would like to also recognize the wonderful book, A Shepherd Looks at Psalm 23, by W. Phillip Keller as one of those influences in my life. His book opened my eyes and many others to the loving, intimate, caring Shepherd God that we have been invited to join, as sheep in His pasture. May Keller's faithful words continue to draw God's family into the close proximity that we are invited to. May we all experience the Good Shepherd's nurturing love in a deeper way.

To His glory,

Rocky

1 | The God I *Need* to Know

When do we really get to know God, or how He sees us?
Oh, I know that most Christians think that we know Him.
We have a concept of Him ... some kind of concept. But
do we really know God? Is our concept of God some-
thing we made up, or something that we pieced together
from multiple sources? Do we pick and choose aspects
of Him that we like and discard those that we don't
like—or don't understand—and say, "That is God and
I know Him!" Is our concept of God accurate when we
do this? Do we really know Him if we do not know His
heart, His ways, or even how He sees us and loves us?

How about the multiple teachers and sources, and their
concepts that caused us to form our concept of God?
Are they accurate? Is our information coming from
books, from sermons, from teachers, from philosophers?

*Are all of these sources reliable? Any of those sources
could be skewed because of bias, which could result in
an incorrect concept of God. This skewed concept of
God can be as easily reproduced as one that is accurate
to another person and we miss a true perspective of
God. If this happens there is much at stake and much
could be lost. Are you willing to risk the Treasure that
could be yours by not truly understanding God?*

*How about philosophy? Have you manufactured a con-
cept of God based on someone's educated ideas about
God, or have you even used your own philosophy to
construct a concept of God? Be very careful using these
means to understand God, for everyone has his or her
own philosophy, and most philosophies are skewed one
way or another. So how do we understand God? How
do we get the best view of the most powerful and loving
Entity that has entered the world and our life?*

*The truth is there is only one way to get a correct view
of God, and to have an accurate concept of Him. It is to
study what He has revealed about Himself, and the most
accurate source of these revelations is the Bible—specifi-
cally what we see in Jesus. Why Jesus? How do we understand God by understanding the Man/God called Jesus?
Here is what scripture says about that question:*

"The Son is the radiance of God's glory and the exact representation of his being, sustaining all things by his powerful word. After he had provided purification for sins, he sat down at the right hand of the Majesty in heaven." (Hebrews 1:3 NIV)

Get that? Jesus is the exact representation of God. When we get to know Jesus—really get to know His nature, His perspectives, His demeanor, and His values—we get to know God. Therefore, to know God accurately, we need to know Jesus intimately and we need to make it our priority to seek this intimacy with Him and get to know God through Jesus. This close proximity allows His Holy Spirit to affirm what we read about Him, as He leads us to the truth about who God is. However, sometimes God will use one of His children who is inspired by His Spirit to show us how to hear God and be taught by His ways, which was the case in my life. God gave me just such a man to be my mentor and help me seek and find answers to a question that I've had for a long time: "What is there about God that I need to know?"

There was something about this man's understanding of God that I was missing. I wanted to get into his insight for as long as he was alive. Most of all, I wanted to

*know if there is a key insight that I could find to unblock
my confusion and put me on the right path to knowing
God. To be honest, I didn't know that what I sought was
even possible until this man opened my eyes to what
was missing. What I sought was revealed, and this is my
story about it. Maybe my story will help you in your pursuit of knowing God ... the God who wants to be known
as He is. I pray that it will.*

Gabe was not a philosopher, though he was very wise
and experienced as an older man. He was not a theolo-
gian, though he had an astute understanding of scripture
and how it should be applied to everyday life. He was
not an evangelist or high-pressured voice trying to im-
pose his personality or understanding on anyone, though
he was willing to gently reveal insights that made a
person stop and think. He invited me into his life. He
was likable and transparent, which are qualities that
make a man approachable. Best of all Gabe didn't
spoon-feed me answers. He made me seek answers for
myself and dig up treasure from God's Word that caused
me to discover firsthand what God is like. He did this
purposely, for he wanted my faith to be birthed by God,
sustained by God, and used by God to help others find
Him. Gabe was simply a messenger. He was my mentor
and he kept my eyes pointed toward Jesus, looking for

answers to my questions. Perhaps that is why I am now a messenger of the truths I've learned.

After I first got to know Gabe it was my practice to drive to his farm to see him as often as possible before he passed away. We both loved each other's company. It was about two years after the snowstorm that sent me to his front door asking for his help that I was with him again for a weekend. Most of our times before this weekend were relaxed and gave me an opportunity to help the old man with some of his chores and enjoy just hanging out with him. I had become a kind of adopted son, at least that is how I saw myself. Since Gabe's children didn't live near him and my father had died several years before, I was longing for a godly older man to be in my life and Gabe had an opening for another kid, even though I was in my forties and he in his eighties. He was a God-send to me. It was on this particular trip that Gabe asked me the question that I asked you. He looked at me over his reading glasses and asked slowly, "What is your concept of God?"

Taken back, I stuttered out some stupid answers that sounded like, "Grandfather-like ... Long flowing beard ... Got it started and backed off ... Bigger things to deal with than me ... Scary ... Powerful ... Mysterious ...

Unapproachable … Rule maker … Looking for me to break His rules … Did I say scary?"

After I got my words out, Gabe leaned back in his rocking chair and let out a sigh and said, "You don't have a clue, do you?"

I answered, "That would be correct." We both laughed.

When Gabe gave me his customary smile, he took away the sting of my ignorant answers and said, "Don't you think it's about time you really get to know Him? After all, if you want to grow to a point that you are willing to enter a deeper relationship with Christ and stay there, you have to trust Him more, don't you agree? Now tell me what you really think He's like."

I thought a little more seriously about the question and said, "He's holy—too holy for me to come close to. He scares me. I don't think I really know what He is like."

"Do you know why? It is because you don't know Him the way He really is, and as a result you can't trust Him as deeply as you should. The fact is, none of us can truly trust someone if we do not believe that person is trustworthy. It is as simple as that. If we get to know God as

He really is, then our trust in Him will grow,"
Gabe asserted.

Then he asked, "When you were with me that first
weekend following the snowstorm, you told me you had
a spiritual breakthrough. You said you realized what you
needed to do, and you took a step in faith to do it. At that
point you were ready to go all in with Him. Is that the
essence of what you told me?"

I nodded that it was. Gabe then asked, "What happened
after that?"

I was faced with answering a question about something
that had bewildered me. The fact is, I was earnest in
my commitment, but I was going in and out of a deeper
connection with Christ like it was a revolving door. I
would come to a point of surrender and go in, only to try
to take back control when something scared me. I was
missing something but didn't know what. I told Gabe
that this was what was happening. He then began sharing
things that helped me see what was missing in my understanding. He started his explanation with these words:

"Don't confuse the dedication of your life to Christ with

His transformation of you into the man He is making
you. The transformation of your life as a disciple of
Christ begins after you make a true dedication of your
life to Him. You did this. From that point you have been
tested, and these tests will help you grow in your trust
in the Lord. You will take steps forward and fall back
several times before you get traction to keep moving
forward. Eventually you will grow in your trust of Him
in this process. Your deeper trust moves you closer to
Him, and this is where major transformation of your
life takes place. God is always working in us through
our circumstance to grow our trust in Him so that He
can conform us to His character. It takes time. Don't be
surprised or discouraged that you are in and out in the
early stages, for you are in a growth process. The good
thing is that you have dedicated your life to Him, and it
is His plan to take you beyond that point. However, fear
will need to be removed from you, or you will stagnate
in your growth."

"How does God remove my fear?" I asked.

Gabe answered, "In your vision you were told that
your fear is directly impacted by your trust in God; is
that right? If you haven't thoroughly learned that God
can be trusted, then you will not thoroughly trust Him,

will you? Entering the Inner Chamber of intimacy with Christ will require personal abandon and absolute trust. We can say at one time that we did it. But our abandon and trust are not one-time things that we do. They require an ongoing surrender of our fears and our illusions that control our life to remain in the intimate trusting state with Him. We must place less dependence on our illusions of control and replace them with the certainty of God's control. If we want to enjoy the peace that living under God's sovereign authority gives us, then we have to trust that He is in control. There can be no conflict about this within us. That is why the Holy Spirit is at work to grow our trust in Him all the time. It is for our own good."

I asked, "Gabe, I see this and agree with what you are saying. My question to you is how can I get to know Him better and trust Him more? I see it in you. How did it happen for you? Surely you were once where I am now? What was the key that unlocked the door for you?"

Gabe answered, "Like I said, you've got to get to know how God really is if you are going to trust Him more deeply. If you want to know what opened my eyes and heart to the God that I didn't know when I was where you are right now, it was building a solid foundation with my perspective that God is trustworthy. Let me suggest that this is what we pursue this weekend. Let's build a foundation for you to understand God better and help you trust Him more. Then we can see if that begins to take away some of those fears that keep you from remaining in a trusting relationship with Him. Do you want to do this?"

I cannot tell you how this encouraged me. I was given hope that there was something that could help me understand the God I did not know, and who I needed to know. I answered, "Gabe, I'm all in with this. Just tell me what to do."

Gabe answered, "Let's start by firing up Old Bessie, cooking supper, having a good meal, and then returning to the porch to establish the first building blocks in your foundation." I knew Gabe was talking about his old wood stove and the amazing meals that have been cooked on it. My mouth began watering from that point, for I knew it would be something good.

God's Character-
2 | The Foundation of
Trusting Him

I never had a bad meal that Gabe cooked. He was an
artist in his kitchen, which was primitive but did not
limit his skills as a chef in any way. I think he could
have cooked anything he wanted to attempt with his
customary excellent fashion. Very few people would
know how to skillfully use a wood fired stove to fry,
bake, sauté or do anything that could be done on some
of the most expensive cook surfaces or ovens that were
available. Even so, Gabe kept close to his food culture
as a Black, Southern man and I loved it. This particular
night he pounded down and tenderized the steak cutlets
I had brought with me, so they would fry up crisp. After
he had tenderized them, he seasoned them, floured them,
dredged them in a broken egg, and floured them again.
After this he added ground black pepper on the
battered meat and put it in a cast iron skillet to fry

quickly. He also cooked collard greens fresh from his garden, candied sweet potatoes and purple-hull peas that he had grown, and of course his customary buttermilk cornbread. One could imagine the aroma filtering through the kitchen.

Some people would call what Gabe cooked "soul food," found primarily within the African American culture. He explained to me that it was actually survival food when his people were enslaved and mistreated. Instead of the choice parts of the meat provided, they were given the less desirable parts of animals to survive on. This is where slow smoking and cooking made those parts such as ribs, hearts, liver, and intestines, as well as wild game, become a part of their food culture and loved by many of us. Most of the greens and other vegetables they cooked were brought by them from Africa and made their way into the American culture, especially in the South. I told him that I was also exposed to the same dishes by my grandparents and family growing up. He asked me if my grandparents went through the Great Depression, which they did. He said they too had to create survival food just like his people, and that is why I was exposed to it. In both cases we shared a love for common dishes. Personally, I've come to identify "soul food" beyond the Black culture. It might not be fully understood or embraced as it should be, for it is not just about particular dishes. Some people will call it something else, but at the heart it is identified in all cultures as "comfort food." It is a food people grew up with, that they identify with the culture they grew up in. Those special dishes summon good memories from our past. I think both comfort food and soul food have the same intention, which is to nurture someone more deeply than just bodily nourishment from the food. It's about family, friends, laughter, and the joy of eating. There are different dishes, but the same intentions. Gabe's meals offered to me by my loving and gracious mentor nourished my soul, as well as my body. I felt my soul was comforted by this man and his food. His food was true soul food in the deepest way to me, for it was a gift from Jesus through Gabe to me, and it went to my soul by way of my stomach. This made me think that no matter what we give someone in the name of Jesus— whether it is food, drink, or other acts of love—we are nourishing their soul.

When I was thinking this thought, another thought came to me—could I too have a "Gabe" in me that could nurture someone else's soul as Gabe was doing for me? Maybe not in the same way, but with the same motivation and providing the same impact? I sensed that Gabe was being used by God to show me the way to the sustaining intimacy with Christ that I desired, and how this will lead to more things because of it. Indeed, Gabe's meal was a good way to start building my understanding of the God I didn't know. Gabe was serving up more than food to me as he set the stage.

After our meal and my washing the dishes, Gabe and I took two plates of pecan pie and cups of coffee to our rocking chairs on his porch. I followed him out. He had his Bible on the small table between the chairs. After we ate the pie, Gabe opened his Bible and read a verse to me:

"The glory that you have given me I have given to them, that they may be one even as we are one, I in them and you in me, that they may become perfectly one, so that the world may know that you sent me and loved them even as you loved me."(John 17:22-23)

Gabe asked, "Did you know this was a prayer from Jesus to Father God about you?" I leaned into Gabe's words, for it surprised me that such a prayer would be given for me by Jesus. Gabe continued, "Jesus was asking His Father to give to those of us who follow Him the same intimate fellowship that He had with the Father. What do you think Jesus's view of His Father God was?"

I had never thought of it that way, nor had I made a connection that Jesus had made available for me the same relationship with the Father that He had. So, I had to think through what Jesus had taught about God, and the things I understood about a good father. A good father's love would be tender, nurturing, encouraging. He would be concerned for his child all the time. He would lovingly discipline his child for his or her own good. He would be attentive. He would be committed. After I quickly processed those aspects of a good father, I shared them with Gabe.

"I agree with your thoughts on this." Gabe continued, "These are the characteristics of a good father. However, no matter how good we are as human fathers, we are limited by our knowledge of our child in every circumstance and occasion. We are still human and subject to imperfect human feelings that might cause us to be reluctant to be involved in all situations or circumstances even if we knew them thoroughly. After all, our love is not perfect all the time. This is true for all humans. We always disappoint someone in some way. We even disappoint ourselves, for we are not perfect.

"We might be willing to overcome our hurt or angry

feelings toward our child because we are a good father. Even so, we may still be unable to help our child for we are limited with our ability to help. We may lack the resources, and we would also be limited by our incomplete knowledge of what is right for our child to help him or her. There are a multitude of limiting factors that we will face, even though we are a good father. No matter how good an earthly daddy is, he is still limited as a human father because he is only a man. This is not true with Father God. He has none of those limitations, and this is where you start building your foundation of trust on the true God. You've got to see God as He is, and not superimpose a false picture based on second- and third-hand information, or a philosophical belief. Father God is perfect in His love, for He is perfect. His love cannot be achieved by any of us, no matter how hard we try. His knowledge is complete about us, and His ability is unlimited. We try to humanize Him to understand Him. But we will fail to understand Him this way, for we have only earthly comparisons to use and they fall short. He is much, much better.

"I asked you what your concept of God is. There is only one true concept of God, and that is the truth of who God is and not a concept that a human mind imagines. Therefore, you must empty yourself of the multiple images and identifiers of God that have filtered into your mind for many years and use only one source to see Him as He is, which is the Bible. So, let's begin by letting me give you an illustration to make a point."

Gabe then walked down the steps of his front porch and then to the side of the house. Once he got to the place he was taking me to, he pointed to four brick pillars that supported the foundation on that side of the house. He asked me to explain what I was seeing. I told him about the four pillars. He then asked, "What are the pillars placed on?" I looked and couldn't see anything, for they seemed to go deeper than the soil's surface. Even though he had heard me respond to his question, Gabe didn't answer my observation. He simply asked, "Look under my house and see what is placed on the brick pillars." I looked and could see a heavy wood beam. To complete the point he wanted to make to me, he asked me what was on the heavy wood beam. I told him the floor and house. After these questions and me seeing what he was referring to, we went back to the front porch to make the connection that Gabe wanted to reveal to me.

"Let's read a scripture where Jesus speaks of the necessity of a good foundation." He then turned in his Bible to Matthew 7:24-27 and read:

"Everyone then who hears these words of mine and does
them will be like a wise man who built his house on the
rock. And the rain fell, and the floods came, and the
winds blew and beat on that house, but it did not fall,
because it had been founded on the rock. And everyone
who hears these words of mine and does not do them
will be like a foolish man who built his house on the
sand. And the rain fell, and the floods came, and the
winds blew and beat against that house, and it fell, and
great was the fall of it."

He then said, "I showed you the foundation of my house
to make a comparison with the way God builds a
foundation under you. Jesus speaks of just such a foundation. As there are four brick pillars that support the
large beam that supports my house, there are likewise
four characteristics of God that I will show you that
support His relationship with you. Just like the beam
connects to the foundational pillars for the house and
supports it, your faith connects you to God's characteristics that support your life. Your trust in those four
foundational promises that God has made joins His
truths to your life and He will then form your life on top
of it. This is the life built on the solid foundation that
Jesus speaks of. The four characteristics of God that

I will mention along with the foundation under each characteristic will give ample reason to trust Him. Do you understand the comparison I am making?"

As I thought about his question, I was shown some things about a foundation for a house that I was not aware of. I could see how it was all joined together to support the house that is built on it. The truth is, we most often look at a house and are rarely concerned about the foundation, and yet it is the most important aspect of the house. When the foundation of the house fails, the building on top of it fails. I understood that Gabe wasn't teaching me about the construction of a house but rather the construction of a life. He was giving a convincing illustration that a life requires a good foundation, and how it is built determines how that life turns out. I told him that I understood where he was headed but needed to know more. He had more to say.

"My daddy and his daddy built this house over a hundred years ago. They cut the timber off the property to make fields for grazing the animals. They took the trees to a local sawmill and bartered labor and crops to have the wood cut into lumber and beams for the house. They built every part of it. They were master carpenters and that is why the house still stands today and hasn't shifted a bit since being built. The most important part is the foundation that supports the house, and they spent a lot of time getting it right. I asked you about what was beneath the brick pillars. You said you could not see it. What is beneath and out of sight is the most important part of the foundation. You see, the builders dug down through the soil until they hit bedrock, and on the bedrock they poured concrete to place the brick pillars on. You can't see it, but it is there. That bedrock serves as the foundation for those pillars and everything above it. The bedrock gives the most important and strongest support for the entire house, for the bedrock doesn't move. Likewise, there is a major support characteristic of God that holds up everything else above it. It has to be the strongest support in your foundation, for with it all things are held together and built on top of it. This bedrock for your life was established way before you entered your relationship with Christ. It is how you were joined to God in the first place."

Gabe then paused and waited for my thoughts to catch up. I knew there was something special about the bedrock he was illustrating. He pulled it together. "To deeply trust God, you have to understand the way He loves you. His first effort to reach out to you and to build a foundation under you like the bedrock I speak of, was to give you a foundation of grace. Your relationship with Him began and will complete with His grace to you in Jesus Christ. I repeat—your relationship has started, will sustain, and will be completed by God's grace to you. On this most important characteristic of God, your life with Him and for Him will be built. It is the immovable base that supports everything else about Him that I'm about to show you. You must remember this, for it will comfort and guide as you move forward."

3 | The Bedrock of *Grace*

When Gabe spoke of God's grace being the immovable base in my relationship with God, at first it shot over my head and didn't have the impact that it should have had. Like so many Christians, I didn't really understand the broadness of God's grace. I was well schooled in how my sin separated me from Holy God. I lived with that struggle even as a Christian. I understood that it took God's unconditional love to save me. I believed this. I had asked Jesus into my life because of it. That part of grace I understood. Beyond that, I was in the dark. So, I asked:

"Gabe, I understand that it is by God's grace that I am saved. I know there is nothing I can do to earn my way to heaven and that by God's grace He sent us Jesus. But what am I missing?"

The old man leaned back in his chair and said, "Identifying your relationship with God by His grace to you will give you a perspective to look through for the rest of your life. God told Paul that His grace was sufficient for everything he would face."

This last comment reminded me of the passage that spoke of Paul's thorn in the flesh and how he had asked God to remove it. The Lord told Paul that He would not remove it for His grace would be sufficient. I had to be honest with Gabe and ask a question that had bothered me for a while.

"Gabe, you speak of God telling Paul that His grace would be sufficient. I've talked to a lot of people about this and it sounds like God told Paul that he had to be satisfied with His grace rather than an answer to his prayer. I have to be honest and say that I don't understand why God would short change Paul by giving him a minimum just to get him by." After I said this, I felt that I shouldn't be critical of God. But I had to be honest with Gabe.

Gabe listened and nodded while saying, "I know it looks that way for those who do not understand or appreciate

God's grace. That is why you need to understand it better. Then you will understand how God's grace extends further than you can imagine and do more than you would ever envision. God was not giving to Paul the least of His blessings when He told him those words. He was telling him that He was giving to him the best He has to offer. You see, God's grace is sufficient because it comes from God, and contains all that God can do. Like the bedrock is immovable, unchangeable, and able to support my house, God's grace is all of that for supporting a life built on it."

"How does that work?" I asked.

"To begin with, it helps you embrace a perspective that will remind you that you've done nothing to deserve God's forgiveness of your sins, or by your works to earn a place into His family. It is His unconditional gift of grace extended to you and received by your faith in Him. This constant recognition of His grace to you will filter into other aspects of your life. For example, when you are tempted toward self-condemnation because of your mistakes, God's grace will remind you that His love stands steady beside you to forgive you and empower you to change. When you are tempted to condemn or slander someone else, God's grace will remind you that

His grace has forgiven you, and you are to do the same for others. God told Paul that His grace is sufficient for anything he would face. It is the same with you and me. When God gives us His grace to live by, He is giving all that grace includes. It is the most important and complete gift for helping us live our life and to face every circumstance that we could ever have. It is God's best to us. There are so many other aspects of grace that will be used to teach you, to lead you, to empower you, and to transform you that I cannot mention them all. I can only say that it is the foundation of your relationship with God, and it will support your bond with Him from now on."

When I heard Gabe describe it as He did, I understood why he saw it as the first thing I needed to establish in my perspective to understand God better.

Gabe continued, "If you want to understand grace better, you need to understand that there are three points to God's grace that you need to consider. The first point is that you are justified by grace and grace alone. It is not because of your good works, your church affiliation, or how moral you are. You are justified by God's uncon-ditional love, which is His grace. You could not make it without it. The second point is that you will one day be glorified by God's grace when you go to heaven. You will not enter by any other means except by the grace of God that was given to you through Jesus His perfect Son. It will not be because you deserve it. It is by God's grace alone that you will be glorified and go to your heavenly home, and by no other way. However, it is the third point where believers often struggle." Gabe kept me listening intently to hear the third point.

He resumed, "The question is, what about our life between justification and glorification? What about the life we live between being saved and going to heaven? This is a period that has been called our sanctification period. Can a person lose their salvation during this period? Some think they can. I think they have this perspective because they do not fully understand the completeness of God's grace to them. So that you will not be confused, you need to understand the third point of grace.

"Many Christians get it wrong here and they never enter the deeper relationship with God that has been given to them because they hold onto an illusion that they have to work to keep that which was freely given to them or else they do not deserve it. They just do not understand grace. Most Christians agree with the first two points

and will not argue about them. But during the time
between those two aspects of their life they carry a
burden, thinking they have to prove themselves to God
or else He withdraws His grace from them. They might
not realize it, but they are trying to win God's love when
He has already given it to them. They think He will
no longer love them if they sin, for they are confused
about the way He loves. This is wrong for He still gives
His love to us even when we sin, and it is in this love
connection that we begin to conform to His values and
desires. We then begin to sin less. Because of this misun-
derstanding about sanctification by grace, some people
put a self-imposed burden on themselves that God does
not give them. They just do not understand that we are
also sanctified by grace and we all need to learn to walk
in it to be empowered to change. That is the third point.
Just as we are justified and will one day be glorified by
God's grace, we are also sanctified by His grace. Saved,
sanctified, and one day glorified by God's grace. Our need
is to learn to walk in this grace and it will walk us into
becoming the men and women that He wants to form."

When Gabe made this point, it all began it make sense
why I had been so scared of God and didn't really trust
Him. I needed to understand Him better by understanding His grace better. I had this mixed-up works-oriented

perspective that looked at myself and could clearly see why I couldn't be loved, and this made me think I had to work to get and keep God's love. Understanding the way God loved me would one day shatter this false message and the legalistic burden that I carried. However, right now I could see that I was missing an understanding of the way grace sanctified me. Gabe told me that God's grace to me was the first characteristic of God in my foundation. I could see that I was not recognizing God's grace as I should, sadly. I could embrace the gift of salvation by grace alone. I understood this. But there was this hidden voice that kept saying to me, "You now have to prove yourself to God. He will leave you if He really knew you. He's given this gift of love to you and now it's up to you to keep it." I can now see that this voice came from the Accuser. It was certainly not the voice of God.

I told this to Gabe, and he said that he was once hearing that same voice until he began to understand the bedrock of God's grace that held him up. When he began to stand on God's grace to him, the Accuser's voice was drowned out by God's voice. Gabe shared what he felt God had spoken to his heart:

"I know your weaknesses, and I still love you. I know

*your struggles and I want to help you overcome them. I
will not discard you. I will guide you if you will listen to
Me ... if you will trust Me. I know first-hand the tempta-
tions that you face. I've been there. I know what they feel
like. But I overcame them, and I will help you overcome
them as well. Never think that your failures keep Me
from loving you. I have you in My grace at all times, and
My grace will never let you go. Learn to live in and walk
by it and you will become the man I want to
make of you."*

After Gabe told this to me, he asked, "Which voice do
you want to listen to? If you follow Satan's voice it will
lead you into despair, condemnation of others and
yourself, and the darkness where Satan wants to take
you. But if you follow the voice of our gracious God, it
will lead you to becoming the man He wants to make of
you, which is strong and courageous, tender and
sensitive, like Jesus. You have to stand on God's grace
when the voice of the Accuser comes at you. It starts
right there and grows you to a closer walk with Christ."

When my thoughts centered on what I did not understand about God's love for me, I then began to see how
I needed this foundation that Gabe had been speaking
of, in order to fathom the other things missing in my

understanding of God. Gabe was a wise mentor to start with this first building perspective in my foundation. From that point on he unfolded more insights about God's character that would walk me to the answer that I was seeking. It is the question that we all have and we all need to answer if we will allow God to lead us. The question it comes down to, that we will need to ask and find an answer to is, "Can God be trusted?"

4 | God's Knowledge of *Me*

After Gabe had laid the undergirding foundation of
grace, like a skilled mason he laid one of the foundation pillars on it. He began by taking me to Psalm 139
and had me read it. He asked me to underline any verse
that spoke of God's knowledge of me. When I pointed
out a verse, he asked me to tell him how the promise in
the verse made me feel. I saw quickly the whole chapter
was about this assurance that God knows me thoroughly.
The first revelation was seen in the first six verses. I
pointed it out to Gabe and he then asked me how the
passage made me feel. I answered:

"The passage points out God's knowledge of me and
tells me that he searches me and completely knows me.
To me this means that the things other people cannot see
in me, including my own earthly family, are not hidden

from God. His knowledge of me is totally thorough, which is not the case with all my other relationships."

I continued, "Next, I read that I am never out of God's sight. Concerning God's knowledge of me, He even knows my thoughts. I am told He knows where I go during the day and when I sleep at night. He knows all things, everything about me. I read that He even knows my words before I speak them.

"I liked the thought conveyed in verse 5 that God hems me in before, behind, and has His hand upon me. It gives me a mental picture that I have God's complete protection on and around me all the time. The thing is, if I would truly believe this, I think it would give me the courage to face each day and all the challenges that come at me."

"How so?" Gabe asked.

"It tells me that I'm not alone, and God is right there with me. It's kind of like a child surrounded by bullies. If he is alone, he is frightened. But if his father stands next to him, he feels safe and secure. If I feel that way about God's presence in me, would it not make me have greater peace in challenging situations?"

My mentor didn't respond, for the truth had been seen by me and its implication was taking root. Instead he answered me indirectly.

"Tell me how these characteristics of God make you feel right now."

"I feel comforted with a hope I didn't have before. I feel safer. Like it was with David, my understanding of the complete knowledge that God has of me is more wonderful than anything I can imagine. But it also scares me. I am told that I cannot hide anything from God. He knows all my sins, my thoughts, my issues, my wounds, my junk, and this shakes me." Gabe nodded in agreement with a serious expression and said:

"In every instance, those people who have come into God's presence have been frightened. They were shaken to a point near death, and for good reason. He is awesome, powerful, and in many ways He is frightening. But this limited view of God doesn't give us the complete picture of Him, and that is why God became a man and walked among us. He wants us to relate to Him in a way that we can understand as a human, so He sent us Jesus. When we see and understand the characteristics of Jesus, we see a complete picture of the character of God.

"You mentioned your fear because of God's complete knowledge of you. Of course, we all do things we are ashamed of. If God were just a fair God, then He would demand justice and we would not measure up. His knowledge of us would charge, convict, and sentence us because no fact would be unknown by Him and we would deserve His punishment. But there is another characteristic of God that needs to be understood: He is merciful. This means that even though He knows when we sin and are disobedient, He doesn't use His knowledge against us. He gives us mercy because He is a merciful God, and not because we deserve it."

When Gabe told me about the merciful characteristic of God, I felt relief. He went on to say:

"Those characteristics can also be seen in good earthly fathers as well. We know this, for we know some people like that. They are rare, but they are out there. However, what they cannot give as earthly fathers is perfect love, which is what God does. This is something you need to understand about God if you want to build a foundation of stability in your trust of Him. Undergirding God's knowledge of you is the bedrock of His grace, which is perfect, unconditional love. God gives His children grace, which is totally underserved by us. It is the perfect love of God that cannot be compared with any earthly examples.

"You must understand better what this grace is and learn to walk in it to stabilize your trust in God and His knowledge of you. His grace will teach you about who God truly is and you will then begin to see Him as He is. His grace will teach you how deeply loved you are by Him, and you will begin to see yourself differently. His grace will eventually flow through you like a river of water, and you will see other people differently. God's knowledge of you and your mistakes will not be used against you because of His grace, and it will be His knowledge of you that will be used to help you.

"Some people would ask if leaning too heavily on God's grace makes Christians lazy or less involved with serving other people. If this happens it is because they do not really understand God's grace or the stewardship of His grace to them. Understanding and living by God's grace enables us to represent Him in the best way, for His grace flows through us to others. It is Christ to us, Christ in us, Christ through us, and Christ to others. If

we stop up His grace in our life and not allow it to flow
to others, our relationship with Him will be hindered and
we will not understand the purpose that God has given
us. This is why we need to go to the next foundation
pillar and understand another important characteristic of
God. He has a deep concern for what He knows about
us, and He wants to help us for He cares."

This thought about God's care for me was comforting.
I continued to share additional verses from Psalm 139
with Gabe that pointed out God's complete knowledge
of me, from my birth to my future death and all points
between. By the time I completed my explanations of
what I saw in the scriptures about God's knowledge of
me, I was thinking to myself how David's writings in the
Psalm said just what I was feeling. He said the thoughts
God had about him were overwhelming, but precious
to him. I felt the same. It was a strange new feeling
even though I couldn't grasp it. This made me want to
understand God better. There was still a nagging feeling that made me fear His complete knowledge of me.
I was beginning to question if this fear I felt about His
knowledge of me was something God wanted to remove.
There had to be more that would help me understand
how to answer this question.

5 | God Cares About *Me*

When Gabe spoke of building a foundation of trust, I didn't initially understand that he was talking about the character traits of God being the foundation I needed. It made sense to me that we cannot trust someone completely if we do not know them thoroughly enough to know if that person is worthy of our trust. For me to go toward God in and beyond my initial entry into my relationship with Him, I was being asked to trust Him in the deepest way possible. I didn't know where Gabe was headed with the next pillar in the foundation that he was speaking of, but I was intrigued.

Gabe and I finished our coffee and pie and he was beginning his slow movement in the rocking chair to continue our conversation. It is strange how one's body language can create various responses in others such as fear,

caution, alert, trust, or peace. Though we can read about
Jesus' words and actions, we can't see His body
language when He spoke. There is not much mentioned
about that. I only know from the Bible that He mesmer-
ized the people with His communication skills and I think
He used all means to reach the hearts of the people who
saw and heard Him—including His body language—
provided they wanted to be reached. He invited them in.
Even today His words invite us in. Little wonder that a
man who walked with Jesus like Gabe would also be a
skilled and an effective communicator…but in his own
way. Gabe invited me into his wisdom, and the way he did
it was to give me a safe place to go and be led to God's
truths. This safety and the relaxed way Gabe communi-
cated with me spoke volumes about the way Christ would
have taught.

Another factor that influenced me was that I knew
Gabe cared for my soul. He had a serious commitment
to nurturing me toward a deeper intimacy with Christ.
Therefore, it really hit the mark for me when he said
something that addressed the continuing fear I had of
God's complete knowledge of me when he said:

"While it might be a shock to come to understand that
God can know us so thoroughly, it can also be of great

comfort. He knows everything about us…everything.
That kind of knowledge could be dangerous if someone
didn't know how to use it. No human could handle the
responsibility with how to use it for or against someone,
and it scares us to think that God could use it against us.
Therefore, we need to again go to the next characteristic
of God. Read this chapter in the Bible and tell me how it
strikes you." Gabe opened his Bible and turned to Psalm
23 and I read it. I responded to Gabe's question and said:

"I read in this Psalm that the Lord is my Shepherd and
His care for me is obvious. I don't know much about
sheep and shepherding but it sounds like God is compas-
sionate and that was the point David was making."

Gabe said, "Let's read another passage to understand
what kind of shepherd God is, for there are good and
bad shepherds. Here is what Jesus said about Himself
in John 10:14, and remember that Jesus is the perfect
representation of God:

*"I am the good shepherd; I know my sheep and my
sheep know me."*

Gabe continued, "How does this make you feel about
God's knowledge of you? Do you think He will use His

knowledge about you against you or for your good? Do you think it is because you are good and you deserve it, or do you understand that it is the character of God that makes Him care about what He knows about you?" Without pausing, Gabe continued to reveal insights about God and His care for His sheep.

"When David used the metaphor that God is a good shepherd who cares for his sheep, he wasn't far from the truth about the nature of sheep and humans being similar. You see, sheep are self-destructive. They can't fight. They have no way to defend themselves against predators. They easily panic. They will eat the grass below their feet until there is nothing left, and then they starve. They would rather drink filthy, stagnant water than drink from fresh, running water because it scares them. They are peculiar and get themselves in trouble because they ignorantly stray from the shepherd. They are easily misled by something that looks good. They could not survive without a shepherd managing them. Like sheep are dependent on their shepherd for their safety and security, we are also dependent on our Shepherd God.

A shepherd understands that his sheep cannot get a healthy rest if they are afraid. They will get sick or be killed from stress, parasites, predators, starvation, and many other things because they are basically self-destructive. They require a shepherd because they cannot protect themselves. They can even get so loaded down with a heavy coat of wool and debris that simply turning over in a wrong spot on uneven ground can flip them on their back and would stay there until they died. If that happens, a shepherd has to find this sheep, turn it right side up, remove the heavy coat, and get it on its way. A good shepherd has to keep watch over his sheep all the time for his sheep to survive. Even bad shepherds do this to a degree, for they would lose income if the sheep died. However, there is a difference between a good and bad shepherd and you can spot it in the sheep and the land they live on."

"What is the difference?" I asked.

Gabe answered, "I tell you what. It is too late right now, so let's go on a little field trip through the valley tomorrow after breakfast. I will give you some examples of a good shepherd and a bad shepherd by showing you the condition of the land and the sheep that live on it. Then I think you will understand better what David and Jesus were saying in their illustrations about sheep and good or bad shepherds."

I was getting sleepy after the great meal. So, I needed no further urging to go to bed. Gabe and I went to our separate bedrooms and before long we were both snoring.

6 | The Good & The Bad
Shepherds

The next morning after breakfast we loaded up in Gabe's old truck and drove a few miles down the road that ran through the valley. The beautiful valley that Gabe lived in was very diverse with crops, cattle, and sheep ranches, so it was a scenic and enjoyable ride for me. Gabe took his big Bible with him, and I knew my lesson would continue using some scripture to reinforce a point he would make. Gabe was always concerned that his advice would be bathed in biblical truths. After driving a few miles, he took a gravel road off the main road and drove back toward the foothills of the mountains. A few miles down the road, he pulled off to the side of the road and stopped the truck. He exited the truck and I followed him out. As he leaned against the hood of the truck, he looked out over the land. The land had two pastures that were dissected by a fence that divided the properties.

There were sheep in both pastures.

Gabe began, "I want you to take your time and have a good look at both pastures and the sheep in them and tell me what your impression is."

I could tell the land was similar in terrain and such. There was no obvious difference in the pastures because of a lack of water and sun, or differences in the ground conditions. But one side of the fence grew rich and luxurious grass and the sheep were full of wool. They appeared healthy, happy, and relaxed. The other pasture was sparse in grass and the sheep looked thin and agitated. They seemed to be unhealthy. I told Gabe my impression and asked why there was a difference. He said:

"The land you are looking at was once owned by two brothers. They were both good shepherds. They worked the land by clearing the trees, and planting and cultivating the best grass in the valley. When they got the land right, they brought in sheep. Like the land, they gave a lot of effort to raising the best sheep in the valley. They cared for the land and the sheep equally. The flock was given everything they would need, especially a lot of oversight with the sheep and the land as well. As a result, for many years good profits were made by both brothers.

Several years later when the brothers died, the land was divided among the two families. One share went to the son of one of the brothers. The other piece was sold to a man in the city who liked the idea of owning sheep and the land, but knew nothing about raising them. Therefore, he hired someone to take care of the sheep and the land. Before long, the owner lost interest and the sheep were completely dependent on the hired hand. Which one of the pastures and sheep do you think are overseen by the son and which one the hired man?"

It was obvious that there was a difference. It appeared that in one pasture the sheep and the land were overseen by someone who knew what he was doing, and who cared about the sheep. The other land and sheep looked neglected, and the person overseeing them had little interest in them. I took a guess that the healthy property and sheep were overseen by the son. Gabe stated, "Pretty obvious, isn't it, that we can spot a shepherd who cares for his sheep?"

Gabe next went to his Bible and had me read in John 10 some verses about a good shepherd and a hireling. He asked me to spot the difference and for me to tell him my thoughts.

"I read in John 10:11 that a good shepherd would lay his life down for his sheep. A hired hand would run away if danger comes. This would leave his sheep alone and vulnerable. In verse 13 it says the hired man runs because he cares nothing about the sheep."

I pointed out something else that I saw in the scripture. "I also read that the sheep know a good shepherd's voice. So, no doubt the good shepherd is trusted by the sheep because they sense he loves them and wants the best for them."

Gabe said, "Those things are true, and it is because of this trust in the good shepherd that his sheep do well. To take care of the sheep and nurture their health, the land they live on must also be nurtured and protected. For this reason, the good shepherd moves the sheep around, so they will not overeat a pasture. If he did not, they would strip the land of its grass and nutrition, and the result would look like that land and those sheep." Gabe pointed to the hired man's land when he said this.

Gabe then pointed to both pastures and said, "We can see there is a difference between the two pastures. One is rich with grass and the other has been damaged because the sheep have overgrazed it. It is obvious that the overseer of the sheep of the damaged pasture is the hired man. Moving the sheep around creates more work for a shepherd, for he has to be among them while he directs them. This requires that he is involved with the move. He has to be with them during this move and it requires his attention and extra effort. Incidentally, the sheep will be more easily moved by the good shepherd for they know his voice, and they know he cares for them. They quickly follow his voice for they are familiar with it. They trust his voice for they trust him. Christians are a lot like that. The closer we are to our Shepherd and the more we are familiar with His voice, the easier it is for us to accept change and to follow Him."

Gabe changed the subject. "Did you note how agitated the sheep were in the bad shepherd's pasture? It is because they are disturbed by insects that get into their eyes and nostrils. Do you see the sheep of the good shepherd agitated?" I said that I did not. Gabe explained, "It is because the good shepherd has treated them with salve that protects them from the irritating insects. The bad shepherd does not treat his sheep for he doesn't care about them. What does this say to you?"

I answered, "It tells me that the good shepherd knows all the needs of his sheep and he takes care of them. He is watching over them, even when they don't understand what is happening. He loves them—and that is the difference between the two shepherds."

"Well said. Now how did Jesus describe Himself?"

"He said that He is the Good Shepherd."

"Do you believe this?" Gabe asked. "Do you believe that Jesus is the Good Shepherd?" I nodded that I did. He then asked, "Do you believe that He is your Good Shepherd? Do you believe that He oversees you and watches over you because He loves you, or do you believe that He is a hireling and doesn't care about you? What you believe about God at this point will be the next foundation pillar with you getting to know God better. It will be placed next to God's knowledge of you, and those pillars are always resting on the foundation of God's grace to you. Do you see the connection?"

Without waiting for my response, Gabe went to the truth of what I needed to understand. "If you do not know that God cares about that which He knows about you, you will be afraid of Him. This is why you are afraid of His great knowledge of you right now. You do not know the deep truth of His heart, and His love for you. You do not grasp it, and this is why you are having a hard time really trusting Him. God has sent you His Son Jesus to show you what He is like. But unfortunately, you look at Him at a distance, as if He doesn't care about you. You must not see Him as the hireling shepherd. You must accept what He has shown to you about Himself and embrace His love for you. You can go no further in understanding Him and loving Him and feeling His love for you if you do not accept this truth that Jesus has revealed to you. He is your Good Shepherd and He cares for you! Will you accept this fact and accept this truth in your foundation?"

It was like a slap in the face to be hit with such a convincing comparison of the two shepherds and the understanding that Jesus revealed about Himself. I felt a loving embrace, almost as if I was picked up by my Shepherd and brought into His arms. Tears began to flow down my cheeks when I understood the reality of how Jesus looked at me. Gabe saw my tears and put his arm on my shoulder and said, "I know the feeling, son. It is overwhelming to get in touch with God's love for us, a love we didn't realize that He has for us. Your tears of realization show me that God is building you a strong foundation to help you to know Him better. There will be other pillars that we will add. Until I share them, it might be good for you to process what's been shown to you so far." With that statement, Gabe and I drove back to the farm. There was still plenty of daylight. When we arrived at his farm, I walked down to the fishing hole behind Gabe's house to spend some time in prayer.

7 | The *Reality* of God's Grace Sinks In

As I settled down by the mountain stream that ran through Gabe's property, I tried to absorb what had been shown to me. The fish were working the water, coming to the surface to snatch a newly hatched insect that had fallen on the water. I wished I had my fly rod. However, I was there for another reason that was far greater than fishing. I wanted to process what I had learned earlier in the day. The fact is, I was gloriously confused.

I was like most people in that I lived by my experiences; and as a result, I was rather cynical that I required proof. I had grown up thinking that I could not get anything for nothing. Nobody could take care of me better than me. The only design for life is the one that I made. If I wanted to own something I had to get out and make it happen. I now was shaken to my core to hear that I am loved without condition and that someone knows my needs better than I do. I was challenged to hear that there is someone who cares for me better than my dearest loved ones, including myself. I loved hearing this. But to grasp those things, I would be required to trust in an invisible God, to experience the reality of all the things mentioned. Man, I was reeling from the thought of this. If it weren't for a man who I greatly respected and who delivered to me this challenge, I would have run out of the valley as quickly as possible. There is something about the credibility of a person of experience who shares things such as Gabe did with me. I could see that what he shared was reality, and his life was a living testimony of it.

I wanted to believe what I had been told. I've never had something resonate so deeply and harmoniously within my heart as those things about God's love for me. "Can it really be like that?" I asked, as I caught myself saying out loud the thing I was thinking. Can God be so attentive to me, and love me like that? If I believe that scripture is truly God-breathed and has been given for teaching, reproof, correction, and training in righteousness as mentioned in 2 Timothy 3:16, will I trust what has been written and allow it to assure me? I have been told that Jesus is the Way, the Truth, and the Life. I read it in God's inspired Word. I made a choice to believe this about Him. This is the basic entry point to God and I took it. But Gabe pointed out in scripture that there is more that I was missing. He showed me things that I hadn't read or connected with, even after years of being a Christian. It was a case of knowing about Jesus, but not really knowing Him. I was being made very uncomfortable with my comfortable believe-ism. I also felt a hope growing in me. It was as if a burden was being lifted from me that I had been holding on to all my life. I didn't know what it was. If I did, would I finally release it?

As I thought on these questions, an image of the inscription I had read over the Inner Chamber doors in my dream that said, *"He Who Enters This Chamber Must Do So By Personal Abandonment and Absolute Trust"* came to mind. I remembered the fear I felt when I first looked at it. That fear was returning, as I considered the reality of what I was being asked to do. As soon as the fear came to me, the lesson I had received that day about God's grace to me and His knowledge and care for me assured me that there is an answer for the fear I was feeling. I had to deliver my fears over to God. I knew this. But I had to release them by trusting Him more. This was the conflict going on in me when I walked back

to Gabe's house. Gabe had mentioned there are more
foundation pillars. I was ready to hear what they are.

8 | God Has *Promised*

Gabe had dinner cooking on Old Bessie when I walked into his kitchen. It was the usual excellent farm cooking that was simple but always good and filling. While he was stirring the ham and beans that he was making, I asked him a question:

"Gabe, I've been thinking about the things we shared about God's character. I believe they are true, although I will say that I don't understand the completeness of God's grace." Gabe responded by asking:

"Do you know why it is important to establish in your mind that your relationship with God is by His grace to you? It is a constant reminder that He initiated your relationship with Him. He chose you and adopted you into His family. You came into His family as an orphan of the world and were made a son. You are now a joint heir with Jesus Christ and a member of God's family. He chose you—you did not choose Him. Never be confused in thinking that it is because you in some way went to Him, found Him, and earned His love. He loved you before you knew Him and invited you to join Him. By faith you took His invitation. At that point you were given the rights of sonship. But you still see yourself as an orphan. That is common with all of us who start our relationship with Him. But the orphan must not remain.

"Your present perspective tells you that you have to fight the world to survive. It is driven by fear. This viewpoint makes many Christians think that the filthiness from their old life is never washed away, even though they are saved and forgiven by God. They just can't believe they can be given something without working for it. Oh, they can know the theology and will say that they believe that their sins are forgiven. They will say that God gave them unconditional love and complete forgiveness. But the truth of how they really see themselves shows when they stumble and fall and try to recover. If their under-standing of His grace is confused, it will show that they feel they have to work their way back to get God to love them again. This confusion keeps them at a distance, for they never allow themselves to fully accept being made clean by repentance and God's forgiveness. I see this in you, and it is why you are having a hard time remaining consistent in your walk with Christ. You stand afar, for you feel unworthy."

"Why is this, Gabe? Why do I do this?"

"It is because you cannot fathom a love and relationship that can be like God's love for you. It is true for all of us. We have to adjust from our old perspectives that life gave us before God adopted us into His family."

I asked, "Gabe, do you still struggle with the old man that you were before Christ came into you?" From my point of view, I thought that he had it all together, so I was surprised when he said, "It wants to rear its old ugly head every now and then. I suppose it is a lifelong battle to not think like the world does and allow some of my old experiences to resurface. This world is full of opportunities to bring back some painful memories. When it resurfaces, I have to have a trump card to pull out and play when I start to think like an orphan."

"What is that trump card, Gabe?"

"It is simple reminder that God loves me beyond my

understanding and He graced me into His family. He
wants me to see myself as He does and allow His
perspective of me to be my perspective of me. This is
the constant reminder I must have to combat
the orphan spirit."

"How does God see you? What do you think His
perspective of you is?"

Gabe paused and looked at me with a twinkle in his eyes
and said, "I think He likes me." A smile then formed,
showing his gleaming teeth when he said, "In fact, we
are friends. He has not only graced me with His love.
He has also graced me with His affection. I think He
sees me as His friend. I know He is mine. Better than
that, I am His son, and He is my Heavenly Daddy. I
think that is His perspective of me as well."

I could see that God and Gabe were friends, and his
image of himself was driven by this belief. I don't think
any orphan could keep his old perspective of his old life
if he were convinced that his adopted father looked at
him as Gabe had described. I could see that grace is total
and complete and it needs to be a reminder that is essen-
tial with understanding God's view of us. Grace is also
God's hand to lead us deeper into our relationship with

Him and into a life that becomes more like Jesus.

After we had eaten the simple meal of ham, beans, and cornbread, Gabe and I went to our rocking chairs on the porch. Gabe led me to understand that there was another pillar in my foundation to discover. So that I could visualize my foundation, Gabe reminded me that on top of God's grace to me is a foundation fact of His knowledge of me. Like His grace, God's knowledge is also complete. He knows everything about me. Connected to God's knowledge of me is a foundational fact that God cares about what He knows about me. He is my Shepherd. He knows my condition at any time. The Good Shepherd knows the needs and condition of His sheep and He cares for them. His care is complete, for it is founded on His character of grace. I could see how each attribute of God completes all the ones that follow. Gabe then gave me a vision of another pillar in my foundation that I needed to understand. This pillar revealed to me the nurturing and willing God that I did not yet know.

9 | The *Willingness* of God

As he rocked in his chair Gabe stated, "The next foundation pillar revealing another aspect of God's character is a fact that God has disclosed that He is willing to involve Himself in the things He knows and cares about us. Consider the good shepherd. What if he knew the condition of his sheep and he deeply cared about them, but he was unwilling to help them in the trouble they had gotten themselves into? Would he really be a good shepherd? Is that not a characteristic of the bad shepherd who does not care about his sheep? Remember Jesus said that He is the Good Shepherd and does what good shepherds do. Let's look at a scripture to see this." After he said this, he asked me to turn to Isaiah 46:4–13 and read it. I opened my Good News Bible and read from verse 4:

"I am your God and will take care of you until you are

old and your hair is gray. I made you and will care for you; I will give you help and rescue you."

Gabe leaned back and asked, "What does this promise you, and how does it impact you?"

I thought on the verse and the question. I was reading words from God Himself that He had given in this scripture. God was making a promise in this verse. Immediately a flood of thoughts and questions came to mind as I processed the things I had been taught about God that day. Do I believe that God keeps His promises? If I do believe He does, then what comfort does His promise give to me? I am told that God Himself will care for me. His promise for my care is ever present and into the future. He is willing to care for me even into my old age. He said He will never desert me or forsake me. In every situation I find myself in, whether it is something I foolishly got myself into or a trap laid in my path, God is there, taking care of me and willing to be involved. I am promised that God will rescue me. Like a stranded sheep who has been cast down because of the heavy weight of wool and debris that will surely die unless the good shepherd lifts him up and rescues him, I am promised that my Good Shepherd knows my condition and He will rescue me. His eyes are on me. He watches over me like the good shepherd watches over his flock. Like sheep who cannot defend themselves from predators who seek their life, I am promised that my Good Shepherd blocks their way to me with His very own life. As I thought on the characteristics of sheep, I could see why I act so much like them and need a Good Shepherd. Jesus Christ is that Good Shepherd to me. I just didn't understand the completeness of God's grace to me and what I was given when I first believed. His love is complete, and I have every reason to trust Him. He is completely trustworthy, and I need Him to shepherd me so that I can be led into becoming the man He wants to form of me. After thinking these thoughts, I answered Gabe about the promises I read in the verse and I then explained how it impacted me. "Gabe, somewhere in my past I was taught about the law of cause and effect. Basically, it said for every effect there is a cause and for every cause there is an effect. When I read the verse and thought on it, I could see this rule being lived out."

"How so?" Gabe asked.

"These are some great promises that God has given in this verse. The question is, do I believe them? This is where the cause and effect rule shows up. If I believe these promises are true and if I believe that they are given to me to assure me, then the effects of this will be peace, courage, rest, joy, security, and purpose. But I must believe that God keeps His promises and is trustworthy, in order to trust what He says He will do. So, I have to trust God to receive these things. I am challenged to take my theology from theory to reality to realize the effect that the promises give. This peace and the other things will become a reality in my life, if I will believe these things about God and His promises, and stand on them."

"So, it hinges on your trust in God so that you can trust His promises. Is that right?"

I answered Gabe with a yes. "What is the cause and effect if you do not trust God?" Gabe asked.

"Then I must conclude that my life and those I care for will be safe and secure only if I can make it happen," I answered. "I would have to be alert at all times. I would have to know every situation that might come up, if I am to safeguard against all danger. I would need to know the condition of my loved ones at all times, if I am to be their protector. I would need to know all the ins and outs of the economy to head off financial disaster. I would need to know all the weather patterns to avoid serious storms. I would need to know about the drunk driver on the road ahead of me to prevent an accident. I must know everything that is needed for life, for my future, for all my concerns and an unknown future."

"What can you conclude about this?" Gabe asked.

"It is impossible for me to do all those things. Therefore, I must conclude that total control of my life is an illusion for me or for any other human being. We do not have the capacity or the ability to know all things and be able to safeguard against all possibilities. The cause and effect of realizing this desperate condition either creates fear in me or a need for a distraction to take my mind off of it. However, the older I will get and the more responsibilities that I will carry, the more fearful I will become. There is no distraction from that, for it is reality. I can already see this in my future, because of the cause and effect rule."

"In other words," Gabe said, "you are seeing the reality that no real peace and security for your life and soul can be found by your own means, or the means of the world. The picture of those sheep that were harassed by the flying insects that kept them agitated is a picture

of a soul that doesn't know Jesus as their Good Shepherd. There is a world of harassments and insecurities
that will invade our life, for the rest of our life. We can
have short periods where there seem to be no storms
in our life. But just wait, for one is brewing and coming. It is just a matter of time. God's children will have
their storms and their boat will be rocked liked everyone
else. But Jesus is in the boat with us, and He calms the
storms. He knows the condition of our life, He cares
about those conditions, and He is willing to involve
Himself in those conditions with us. Do you see
the connection?"

I could see that Gabe was methodically helping me reason
through the scriptures the challenges, the false solutions,
and the real solutions. Yes, my eyes were being opened
and the dots were being connected.

Like a skilled surgeon, Gabe had been cutting directly
to the problem of my lack of trust and it was being
exposed. The illusion of my life being under my own
control needed to be faced and removed, and replaced
with the reality that I had been given all those things that
I longed for and could not obtain for myself. The hope
that I had found was because I now realized that God's
character is the foundation of His promises, and His

promises are clear that His grace is sufficient for what I will face at any time in my life. His character assures me that I can trust Him. His character, His grace, and His attributes are the solid foundation that Jesus was speaking of. The cause and effect of getting to know these things about Him convinced me that I was almost ready to let go and trust Him absolutely. However, there was still something holding me back that needed to be addressed.

"Gabe, you mentioned an orphan spirit. Will you tell me more about this? I think something is holding me back from taking what God has freely given to me." I asked this because Gabe had mentioned it a couple of times.

"I will tell you about it later, for it will help you see what might be holding you back. It's the same for a lot of people. So, don't be discouraged. Before I share this, you need to understand that there is another critical foundation pillar in God's character that can make possible any solution for all impossible situations, unless we get in the way. You need to know and believe He has the power to do all things for you that need to be done. He is omnipotent. However, even though this is true about Him, there are things that we can do that can stand in the way of what He is willing and able to do for us. We can, in fact, become our own worst enemy by preventing God's help to come to us. The last foundation pillar is God's incomparable ability to accomplish what He desires on our behalf."

James 4:3

10 | The Hindered Incomparable *Ability* of God

Gabe continued, "So far, it has been revealed to you in scripture that God knows everything about you. His ability to know things about you is inconceivable. No mind or memory that has ever existed on earth can compare with His detailed, intimate knowledge of you.

"To some, this knowledge that God has of them is frightening, for they realize that they cannot hide their sin from God. As an example, the first thing that entered mankind's mind after they had sinned was to try and hide from God, as Adam and Eve did in the Garden of Eden. We still try to hide our thoughts and actions from God. But it is futile. How can we hide anything from Him who formed us, who watches over us, who knows our thoughts and knows what is ahead for us? He knows every turn in the road that is ahead for us. He knew us when we were formed in our mother's womb, when we were birthed, and all our days ahead until we die. This is frightening information unless it is joined with God's compassion. With God's knowledge joined to God's compassion we see a loving, caring God who wants to use His vast knowledge and compassion to bless us.

"He has called Himself the Good Shepherd. Some people do not understand that shepherds were not a glamorous crew of people then. In Jesus' day, shepherds would be in the lower economic class of people. Not many jobs would have been as menial as that of a shepherd. It was hard, dirty work. It was constant. It was isolating. It was in many ways disrespected as a profession, and Jesus compared Himself to a shepherd. Does this speak to your heart as it does mine?

"In some ways this self-perspective that Jesus had makes me love and appreciate Him even more, because I realize that He invaded every class of people to lift up the downtrodden and sober up the prideful. Jesus was the equalizer of men, women, children, the sick, the excluded, and the poor. His love and compassion had no limits. He did not walk to the drum beat of traditions or false religions or social norms. He gave hope to the people then and He gives hope today, for He is the hope giver.

Jesus is a king, the King, who laid down His crown and came to give us hope for the future. He came as a servant and He identified Himself with the lowest of professions to reach to every person, no matter his or her circumstance, and lift them up to Himself.

"Like a shepherd who loves a newborn lamb and wraps it up in a blanket to love and protect it, Jesus lifts us up to love and protect us. He does this because, like His knowledge being inconceivable, His compassion also cannot be compared to anything we have ever known. To understand God, we have to empty our self of all earthly comparisons and see Him as He is. Then our eyes are opened to who He is and what He is to us.

"God has revealed to us by the names ascribed to Him that He is omnipotent. What does this mean? It means He is unlimited in power and ability. He has spoken and separated light from darkness. He has spoken and separated earth from water. He has created everything that walks or crawls or swims. His creation declares His glory, and we will know it if we will look and see it.

"He has told us that our faith in Him will move mountains. He has shown us that His power will invite a friend from his tomb and that friend will obey, for Jesus has power over death. We are told that all our needs will be supplied to us according to God's riches, for He owns the treasures of heaven. He has the resources and the heart to give it to us. God's power can still angry waves and calm the threatening storms in our life, if we will seek His help. I could go on and on about what God's power can accomplish. It is unlimited and it is available for us."

After these enthusiastic words, Gabe paused. The brief pause caused me to rethink the things he had just said about the abilities of God. After a few minutes, Gabe delivered his next statement that hammered home why we sometimes do not see God's help in our life even though we ask may for it. Gabe said:

"As mighty as God's ability is, He can be hindered or limited in being able to help us. We can stand in the way of His help and not receive that which He wants to give us. What a shame that we hurt ourselves when we do this. God is able. The question is … is He able in our life? Do we prevent His help?"

11 | *Removing* Hindrances

Gabe had just helped me see the mighty, unfathomable ability of God. I was now surprised that God could be hindered with anything He wanted to do. It just didn't seem compatible with my perspective about Him. Therefore, I asked, "I don't understand how this can happen. It seems to say that God is not as powerful as I thought. How can He be hindered?"

The old man opened his Bible to the Gospel of Mark and read verses 4-5 in the sixth chapter.

"And Jesus said to them, 'A prophet is not without honor, except in his hometown and among his relatives and in his own household.' And he could do no mighty work there, except that he laid his hands on a few sick people and healed them. And he marveled because of

their unbelief."

After Gabe read the verses he asked me, "In these verses can you see anything that hindered Jesus from blessing the people?"

It was obvious to me that the unbelief of the people hindered Him, for it says that He "could do no mighty work there," because of it. I gave Gabe my answer and he explained:

"Unbelief hinders God's ability to do mighty works in our life, even though we are in His family. It may be a restriction He places on Himself. Nobody really knows a clear answer to this. But it is clear that unbelief or doubt will hinder God's work in our life. However, even a little faith will move mountains, and we will see mighty works of God. In this passage we read about people who Jesus grew up with. It was His hometown. If there were a people that He would desire most to receive what He could give them, it would be these people in His own family and in His own hometown. Even though He wanted it for them, He could not give it to them because of their unbelief. They hindered His mighty works. Do you want to see some more examples?" I nodded that I did.

Gabe then turned to James 4:3 and read it to me: "You ask and do not receive, because you ask wrongly, to spend it on your passions."

"What do you read here that hinders God's power being given to you?" Again, it was obvious, and I said, "Wrong and selfish motives."

Next Gabe went to Psalm 66:18 and read: "*If I had cherished iniquity in my heart, the Lord would not have listened.*"

I answered before he asked, "Holding on to a sinful condition causes our prayers to be hindered."

Gabe responded, "That is another reason that keeps God from giving to us what we ask for. Note the scripture says that this iniquity in our heart is cherished. That means it is valued more than valuing God's opinion of it. It is a desire to keep this iniquity more than our desire to please God. This in itself creates a hindrance that stands in the way of God's best for us, and until it is removed we will not see God's power flowing to our life. Look at this verse. It might hit too close to home." He then turned to 1 Peter 3:7 and read:

"Likewise, husbands, live with your wives in an understanding way, showing honor to the woman as the weaker vessel, since they are heirs with you of the grace of life, so that your prayers may not be hindered."

"What do you see will hinder God's ability to answer your prayers?" Again, it was obvious. If I dishonor my wife and do not show her honor, then my prayers will be hindered. I told this to Gabe and he made an interesting point when he said:

"Just remember your wife is God's gift to you. She is His daughter. You are to love her and honor her and nurture her spiritual life, her self-esteem and her identity as God's daughter. It might be good to remember in this case, God becomes your father-in-law." When he said this last statement, he winked and smiled to add a little humor. Even so, he hit a home-run with me on the point. He had one last scripture to show me how we hinder God's work in our lives.

"Now I want to give you one more verse to consider. Look at what Jesus Himself said of this condition." He turned to Matthew 6 and read the Lord's Prayer. Then he focused on verses 14–15.

"For if you forgive others their trespasses, your heavenly Father will also forgive you, but if you do not forgive others their trespasses, neither will your Father forgive your trespasses."

"What do you see here that hinders God's ability to help you?" Gabe asked. I answered, "Unforgiveness."

Gabe continued, "Yes that is a big one to God. There are many more verses that speak of ways that we can limit God or hinder Him from providing His ability to do things that we ask for. This is why you need to self-feed on God's Word to be made aware of anything that might be hindering your prayers and God's work in your life. If you truly seek to know, He is faithful to help you know what stands in the way."

I asked, "What do I do if I find something that I'm doing that's offensive to God?"

"The first thing is to give it up, turn from it, and seek God's forgiveness. That is true repentance. You can't hold onto it and be repentant. This is where God's grace undergirds our relationship with Him and you can be assured that forgiveness will be given. Look at 1 John 1:9

and see His promise." Gabe read:

"If we confess our sins, he is faithful and just to forgive us our sins and to cleanse us from all unrighteousness," to underscore his point.

I considered the exhortation in John's epistle with how God's family can be restored to unhindered fellowship with Him when we stumble in sin. God is holy, and sin is still offensive to Him even when His child sins. But God's grace is bigger than our sin, and our sin does not destroy our relationship with Him. However, our intimate fellowship with Him can be hurt, and it needs to be restored when we sin. In the scripture Gabe had just read, I could see that God's provision opens His arms and receives us back when we repent. Understanding God's grace as the bedrock in my relationship with Him helped me understand that, even in my sin, God is always providing me a way back to Him, much like the Prodigal Son's father did with his wayward son. I was understanding grace even better and it made me love and respect my Father even more. Is this what happens as we begin to see Him as He is rather than our false perception of Him? Does it make us love Him more? I asked Gabe this question and he said:

"Yes. To see God more clearly and understand Him better causes us to love Him more. I have always seen this to be true in not only my life but in the lives of others who have come to really know Him. However, it is not only our love for Him that increases. Our trust in Him grows as well. It grows because we come to see and understand that He is trustworthy."

I considered Gabe's answer and contemplated my previous and current prayer life. It is true that I have seen many prayers in my life answered in a wonderful way. Some have been delayed, but my problem was eventually worked out and the delays brought hidden blessings I hadn't considered. Some problems that I asked help on were granted, but in a different way than I had considered. It only mattered that it was worked out and the way it was worked out was God's strategy. But there have been some challenges that I did not get God's help with even though I had asked. Most of the problems I brought on myself and, as a result, I had a long struggle to just endure them until I came to understand my mistake. I get it that some prayer requests do not need to be granted, for they are wrong for us, and God protects us by not answering them. There are times that our struggle is by God's design to prune us or sift us. The struggle is actually good for us and eventually becomes a blessing. I've experienced all of those things. However, I never considered that I might be my own worst enemy by hindering God's blessings that He wants to give me. Could it be that I had hindered God's ability to help me in some of those times that I felt He was silent? Did I suffer with the consequences of some of those conditions that Gabe had pointed out because I hindered God's help? Did those unconfessed sins obstruct God's help to me? I resolved from that moment on that it would be my mission to remove any hindrance in the way of God's blessings to me. Life is too difficult to battle without His help and if I get in the way, well, that is not very smart on my part to allow it. I could see that there is nothing more important than fully walking in God's grace and with unhindered fellowship with Him. I was now zeroing in on what my real struggle was with fully trusting Him. But there was more. Maybe the biggest hurdle of all?

12 | The *Orphan* Spirit

Gabe and I called it a day and went to bed early. I was resolved to wake early at dawn and take a walk to process the things I had learned about the four pillars that Gabe had presented to me. Even so, I could not rise before Gabe. He always woke before me and got to the kitchen first to make coffee. I had planned before lunch to drive up the mountain where I had experienced the terrible snowstorm two years before. I wanted to camp out one night before driving back home to get back to the routine of life. Actually, I wanted to do some more processing of the thoughts that Gabe had stirred up, and near a trout stream in the mountains was one of the best places to do it. Gabe told me to take my walk and he would make a big breakfast to sustain me through the day. When he said big, it was an understatement.

As I walked down the gravel road leaving Gabe's house, I remembered the time after the snowstorm that I made a commitment to abandon myself to God and to trust Him deeper than ever before. It was a sincere decision. Things seemed so simple and clear then. I was in an isolated setting. Gabe had been an angel in disguise, and that helped. Like previous experiences, whether they were events or conferences that I had attended before, I seemed to understand more clearly the man that came there and the man who wanted to change. There seemed to be an awakening that made me see clearly what was missing. As a result, I've made many commitments to change and do things better, to love my wife and children better, to lead them to a closer walk with Christ, and to serve Christ better. Even so, my effort was not sustainable. I generally went back to being the same old man when real life issues surfaced. There was a sincere commitment to change. But there was also an inability to hold a true course to life change. Here I was, walking the same gravel driveway that I had walked two years before. It was then that something different happened. I sensed that I had been given a new perspective that would lead me to become the man God wanted to make of me, and it would be sustainable. I was not there yet. But I had a sense that I was a part of some kind of Divine orchestration that would unfold before me.

I also couldn't help remembering the words spoken to
my heart from the Lord that began my journey and led
me to where I was on this road again. I heard then, *"Stop
resisting Me. You are trying to remain the old person,
and I want to make you a new man. You must let go of
trying to keep control of your life and partake of the
Feast in the Inner Chamber."*

As I continued in that vision I came to understand that
this Inner Chamber is a private place very close to
Christ. It was clear that it is there that I will be trans-
formed and become a man that can influence his world
toward Christ. I was truly excited about this prospect.
But, like previous sincere efforts that had gone amiss, I
tried to make it happen with my own effort and shortcut
the process that Christ has laid out. As a result, I
became discouraged.

It was then I remembered the word "resist." I was told by
God to stop resisting Him. Is this what is happening. Am
I resisting Him? What and how am I resisting Him? How
can I go in to this close proximity with Christ and stay
there? Is it even sustainable? What is holding me back?
These were questions that were on my mind and I deter-
mined to discuss them with Gabe before leaving that day.

I went back to the house after my walk and the smells
from the kitchen were tantalizing. I have never gotten
over the smell of food being cooked on a wood fired
stove. I love it. For breakfast Gabe had cooked country
ham, gravy, grits, potatoes, eggs, and pancakes, and
had them waiting for me. When we sat at his table,
he grabbed my hand like he had done so many times
before and began praying for our food. In his prayer, he
eventually began praying for me. When he mentioned
my name, he would squeeze my hand and shake it as if
he were lifting it up to God. I could feel the energy of
his sincere prayer and God's power flow through him
to me. This in itself was a meal for me of spiritual food.
However, the physical food that followed fed my body
quite well. The breakfast was amazing. After we were
done, we walked to the porch with a cup of coffee and
settled into our rocking chairs.

The morning was clear and crisp but would warm up
later in the day, which was typical that time of year.
The spring colors with the dogwoods and redbud trees
were standing out more each day. The fields were rich
with wild flowers and wild onion and garlic plants. The
smells that time of year were sweet and pleasant. The
songbirds were echoing a chorus of songs across the

valley. I had a light jacket on and Gabe was wearing one of his old wool sweaters. The setting offered a relaxed and enjoyable time to talk and take in the morning air, the sounds, the aromas, and to enjoy the view of the farm. Gabe began our discussion by asking me a question. "If you were to describe how you feel right now, what would you say?"

"Honestly, Gabe, I feel some discouragement. I feel that I see this great privilege being offered to me, inviting me to come close to Christ, but something keeps me at a distance. I see that you have it and it is something that I want. But I'm starting to feel that only a few people have it, and I will not be one of them. I understand the characteristics of God that would make me trust Him more. In fact, I do trust Him and agree with all those facts about God that you presented. I even trust Him more because of the way you illustrated things about God. It could not help but open my eyes to the God I didn't know. I have a knowledge of God, but I don't think I really know Him in a deep, personal way like you do. I want to have a trust that never doubts His love or His faithfulness to me. But something is missing in me and holds me back. I don't know what it is." After saying this, I slumped in my chair, finally revealing to Gabe my struggle. I had to admit it to him and myself.

There was a pause in our conversation as the old man allowed my words to linger in the air. He didn't say anything. I felt that he had been waiting for me to get brutally honest with myself about how I really felt, and this pause was his affirmation that I was on the path I needed to be with my honesty. It highlighted the hidden problem that I had and wouldn't admit. He had finally gotten me to a point that he was waiting for. I was now asking the right question which is, "What is standing in the way?"

Gabe finally began talking again. "Have you ever known any orphans, especially those who lived on the streets?" I shook my head that I did not.

"After the war had ended and before I was shipped back to the U.S. I was taken to some of the bombed countries to aid with efforts in helping their people with food, clothes, medicine, and such. They were disastrous places. The wreckage and carnage were horrendous. As a result, there were a lot of children who walked the streets and lived among the rubble, for their parents had been killed. They were living in whatever shelter would provide a warm and dry place to sleep. They scrounged around all day looking for food and warm clothes, just to survive. They were on their own and they knew it. An 'orphan toughness' developed in them. They were tough, suspicious, and extremely cautious. They had a community of other orphan children that they lived with or around. They would have to fight not only the world but each other as well, in order to survive. It was the law for survival. They had to protect themselves first and foremost. Because of the world they lived in, there was little trust that could grow in them. They were just too damaged to trust anyone but themselves. We took food and clothes to them. We had it out on tables to take, free of charge. All they had to do was come and sit down and allow us to serve them … even love them. But many would only come close enough to grab some food and then run like crazy to get back to the rubble where they lived. We had a hard time convincing them that we were not to be feared and that we could be trusted." Gabe paused and took a breath.

"I also served a short span of time in Africa. The children in some of those areas were not in a bombed-out city like Europe. But the same orphan situation existed there as it was in those bombed-out zones. The same distrust. The same running in and out to get the food. The same caution. The same looking out for self. The same survival instincts. You know what I think? I think all of those children, although from different worlds, had a similar perspective that I call the orphan spirit. At the core of this perspective is a feeling that they are unworthy to be loved. Because they think no one could really love them, they would not let their guard down. This bred a feeling that no one could be completely trusted, and they would trust no one but themselves. This orphan spirit made them act in aggressive, distrustful ways to cope with their circumstances to survive."

Gabe continued, "I knew some servicemen who took some of those orphans home with them. They adopted them and brought them into their existing families. They loved them as equally as their birth children. I've heard many stories that these children could not accept a new home and a new life and a new family, for they still carried that orphan spirit with them. They continued to steal their food and hide it, even though it was freely given to them. They kept at a distance, even though love was being flooded over them. They simply would not allow themselves to be vulnerable by trusting someone more than themselves. The main reason was because they had come to see themselves as unlovable, and this would keep them separate from the family. It was only when they would let their guard down and accept the true love being given to them that they could embrace

their new identity as a beloved child. Only then did they
no longer see themselves as unworthy of being loved.
No longer did they see themselves as orphans. They
could then embrace a right identity of being a son or
daughter of their adopted family. Only then did they
accept the benefit of being loved by someone with a love
that they had never known before."

"Gabe," I asked, "this is interesting information, but how
does this relate to me?"

"You remind me of those orphans."

See

I was shocked by Gabe's direct statement to me. He
didn't mince his words. I asked, "Why would you say
that? I have never been an orphan and I don't see how I
could be seen as one. I've never been abused or neglected,
starving, and have never lived a life anything close to
what you have described."

"Oh, I know that is true, just like many men who are
like you. The answer to your question is that you remind
me of an orphan because you see yourself as unworthy
of the love that God wants you to accept from Him. You
know all the theology of God the Father. You have that
nailed down. But I think you still keep God at a distance

instead of embracing Him as your Heavenly Daddy. God sees you as His adopted son that He chose, and He loves you the same as he loves all His other children, and yet you haven't learned to trust His love. The truth is, I think you feel unworthy of His love and you shy away from it, and that is the orphan spirit I speak of. I think you have a hard time accepting God's love, and as a result you try to keep control of your life as a safety net in case God turns His back on you. You have a good grasp of scripture, but you have a big disconnect with your heart and going to a place with Him that accepts a love you cannot understand.

"You can't accept it because it doesn't make sense to you that a holy God could love you like this. You think that He might love someone who was better than you, but not you. You remind me of a starving orphan that's looking through a window at a family gathered around a feast. He sees children that are all happy and eating a great meal around a banquet table. He wants to join them, but he watches at a distance and does not go in. Even though he's been invited to join the feast, he continues to resist. Do you want to know why? It is because he still sees himself in dirty clothes with a tattered life that is filthy with a lifetime of unworthiness. I think you feel unworthy of being loved just like that orphan. Here's the peculiar thing about your perspective: it is because you do love the Lord and respect Him that you will not accept the fact that He has made you worthy of His love. You will not allow yourself to let go of an identity of being unworthy. It is an identity that keeps you beating up on yourself to prove to God that you are grateful that He saved you. This is the orphan spirit."

Gabe was starting to hit a sensitive place in me. I felt a lot of love growing up from my parents and siblings, but I was also wounded by some of the things my earthly father had said. Like everyone, he made some mistakes when handling certain situations. Later I was affected by childhood bullying. Because of these things, I started to toughen up to keep from being hurt any more. I wanted love, but I also didn't want to need it. If I didn't need it, I couldn't be hurt; that was my way of coping. It was something I kept hidden, but Gabe was stripping it away like a bandage hiding an infection. Gabe pulled me out of my thoughts when he said:

"You need to look a little closer at the children around the table celebrating the feast with their adopted father. Look at the pile of dirty clothes outside the door of that banquet table room. All the children were once like you, dirty in their sin from the world they were born into.

They too were orphans, but they stripped off their old dirty clothes and took the clean ones given to them by their adopted father. They left that life and that image of themselves behind and they no longer think of themselves as orphans. They have accepted their adopted father's love just as they are, and he is now affirming them with his love, and it is this love that will reform them into seeing themselves as his beloved children instead of how they once saw themselves. They trust him, for they know he is nothing like anything or anyone that they have ever known. They are there because they accepted his love and adoption and have embraced his affection. I think you still stand on the outside looking in, and that is how you are resisting your adopted Heavenly Father. Until you stop resisting Him and start accepting His love and affection, you will stay as you are. The question is, 'What do you want to do about it?'"

When Gabe asked me this question I didn't know if I was offended or relieved to find a clear answer to what made me resist entering and staying in an intimate relationship with the Lord. At first, I was a little offended that Gabe saw me like he did. Yes, there was an unknown disconnect going on in me. But I hadn't seen myself as having the orphan spirit of feeling unworthy to be loved, although I realized for the first time that I did feel that way. I could see the similarities of an orphan on the streets filtering into my perspective. It was certainly something to pray and think about. Gabe had spoken so clearly about what he was seeing in me that I had to take seriously what the old man was saying to me.

The morning was ending, and I wanted to get on the road before noon. My plan was to go by the general store, pick up some supplies for camping out, and return to the little trout stream I had spent the night by two years ago when the snowstorm erupted. The weather looked good for that night. So, I had no fear that something like a snowstorm would happen again. I went there originally to sort things out and try to determine what I was doing to resist God. I was returning two years later with the same pursuit, and possibly to finally release what I held on to.

I needed to understand what Gabe was seeing in me and there was no better place for me to find it out than by being under the stars, by a stream, and in the mountains. I had been looking forward to this night for a long time. As I walked to the truck, Gabe followed and said, "You know, it is a lot easier to say something to someone that they want to hear than what they need to hear."

I knew he picked up on my mixed feelings about the things he had said to me. I answered,

"Gabe, if you are right and it gets me headed in the right direction then I will be eternally grateful to you."

Gabe answered, "Whether I am right or wrong, you can be sure that it was said in love. I'll just say this last thing. It is easy to spot someone who is struggling with something if you at one time had the same problem. I know where you are, for I was once there as well. I'll be praying for you to find some answers on that beautiful mountain you love so much."

With that last statement I hugged Gabe and loaded up my truck. I headed to the general store and up the mountain soon after. I got to my parking spot a couple hours later, unloaded, and hiked the rest of the way to my camping site.

13 | Sonship

Okay, call me strange. When I go to the mountains to camp out by myself, I go with the basics and look for what I might forage up to eat that might provide a little extra. In other words, I don't stress out about it. When I camped out with my family, I didn't risk relying on foraging for our meals. However, since my children are now in college or have careers that keep them busy, they no longer camp out with me. And my wife said she had enough of it, but has given me her blessing to head to the woods as often as I like. She knows that it is good for me to clear my head, especially since my work is mentally demanding. My camping out also gives me an opportunity to test my skill in foraging. Even so, I bring some basics. My basics on this trip were a big potato, an onion, some butter, salt and pepper, a small grill grate to place over my campfire, an aluminum skillet, and a

small amount of aluminum foil. I also brought my fly
rod. If I would eat any protein, it would be one or two
of the fat trout that lived in the stream by my campsite.
I hoped I would catch something, for a potato and onion
are not much of a meal.

After I parked the truck, I grabbed my camping gear
and headed up a relatively unused trail. That part of
the mountain was unknown to most people, even the
locals. As a result, it was pristine. No trash, no people,
and crystal-clear water. I would be by myself, which I
wanted. I wanted a place that I could pray out loud, sing
without being heard, and weep if I needed it. That place
was an hour's walk from my truck. After an enjoyable
hike, I arrived at my sanctuary.

The parklike setting opened up to a small meadow by
the mountain stream. The pallet of grass by the stream
was only the size of the front lawn of a typical subur-
ban house. There was a large boulder outcropping that
encased the small meadow. When I entered the cozy spot
on the mountain, I felt an excitement that I was like one
of those sheep Gabe had shown me that was frolicking
in the green grass. I immediately went to a spot where I
would build my campfire, and placed some large stones
around an area to create a fire break. I unpacked my

tent and set it up on smooth ground. Before long, those things were finished and ready to use later. It was still early afternoon and I didn't want to catch fish too early, in case I did at all. I wanted them freshly caught and immediately on the grill as soon as possible when they came out of the water. I know it was a risk. But it also gave me an opportunity to rest after the hike, and forage for what I might find around the stream to join the other basic supplies I'd brought.

I decided to drink a little water and take a slight rest. I leaned back against a boulder and fell into a peaceful sleep. As I rested but before I slept, I thought of the impression I had gotten from the Lord two years before, and almost in the same spot I was in now. I had been on a spiritual journey that had led me to understand that I had been resisting God, and He wanted me to let go of something that I didn't know I was holding on to. It was clear that this grip on something was keeping me from moving forward in my journey. Gabe had opened the door to a new thought and he had identified this hindrance in my journey. Do I have the orphan spirit? Do I see myself that way? It was with this last question in my mind that I felt myself dozing off. The last thing I said was a prayer before going to asleep. "Father, if I resist You because I am afraid to need Your love, or

because I think I don't think I deserve it, I ask You to
break through my resistance and walk me into Your
arms. Show me the way, dear Lord."

About an hour later I was awakened by a loud snort.
I looked around to see who it was and realized that it
had been me that snorted. I was glad no one was there
to hear it. But I had to laugh at myself. There was still
plenty of light before I would fish, so I decided to begin
a little foraging close to my campsite.

It didn't take long before I saw a complement to my
baked potato that I had planned. I found some wild
chives, and this time of year I knew they would be
tender and tasty. I planned to chop them up and sprinkle
them on the big spud I brought with me. Good flavor.

As I walked down the stream a bit, I came to some large
sycamore trees. I knew from experience that this was a
welcome habitat for one of the most exquisite edibles
that I could forage up. I held my breath and walked
very carefully around the trees. What I was looking for
is hard to spot. When you find one, there are generally
more. But you have to be careful to not step on them.
It took only a short while before I spotted what I was
looking for. I let out a loud yell of excitement. Popping

up through the leaves like a little golden-brown sponge was a beautiful morel mushroom. Before picking it, and because I had adjusted my eyes to spot them, I saw several other morels around it. I picked enough for supper. I would sauté them in butter to go with everything else. Big addition!

I headed back to the campsite with my forage bag full. I decided to build my campfire and allow the wood to burn down to coals, so I could get my potato baking. After the wood had burned down into coals, I scraped a few coals away with a flat stone and dug a hole in the dirt where the coals had been. I placed my foil-wrapped potato in the hole and covered it up with the hot coals. This process would bake my potato to perfection. I still waited about an hour and then turned my attention to catching a trout or two.

I love fly-fishing. It might not produce the most fish, but it is the most enjoyable and artful way to fish. I love seeing trout in their native habitat tricked by an artificial fly made with horsehair and feathers, or a special colored twine wrapped around a hook. I tie some of my flies and buy some as well. Fly-tying is an art in itself. Depending on what the fish are feeding on determines the fly to use. I looked around to see if there was a hatch that was happening. I looked into the water to see if there was anything floating on or in it that looked like a bug or a midge. I decided to use a nymph, for trout feed underwater eighty percent of the time and the odds were better to catch something.

I got out my fly rod and tied the fly to the tippet. The stream was not very wide, nor did I have a lot of room. So, I used a roll-cast to place the fly upstream to float downstream. After I flew the fly out into the stream, all I had to do was strip the line back to take out the slack and let it bounce on the bottom. When I was doing that I thought, "Well, this is the last thing to get for the menu. If I get it, then I will feast." After a few empty casts, I finally got a hit on my fly rod. By the bending of the rod and the fight going on in the water, I knew I had a big, hungry trout on the line. I played the fish for several minutes before it tired and allowed me to draw him to shore. When I landed the big trout, I realized that it was more than enough for me to eat. So, I laid my rod down and ended my fishing on a high note.

I cleaned the fish, and stuffed chunks of onion and some of the chives in the cavity. I buttered and added salt and pepper to make it ready for the grill. I also washed the morels and got them ready to sauté in butter. Neither dish would take very long to cook. I placed my small grill grate over the coals on some large stones. I then placed my fish and a camping skillet of morels on the grate and allowed them to cook. I turned the fish after a few minutes and stirred the morels in their melted butter. The side of the fish that had been cooked first had taken on a brown hue from the butter I used to coat it with. While the fish and mushrooms were finishing up, I dug up my potato, which was perfectly cooked. I sliced it in half, placed butter on it, and sprinkled some more fresh chives on it. When I finished with the potato, everything else finished cooking at the same time.

With great satisfaction I placed all the food I had cooked on a large aluminum plate that I brought and thanked God for such a bounty to eat. I then dug in and ate until I was completely filled. There could be no finer meal that I could have eaten in the best of restaurants than what I ate that night. I was full. I was satisfied. I was content, and I was thankful. I lifted my arms up to the stars that were now showing themselves in the clear night sky and said out loud,

"Father, Your kingdom declares Your glory!"

I waited a few minutes and prayed, "Your presence is all

around me. Your beauty is obvious to me. Why would I not accept all You want to give me? Why?"

I waited a little while and I felt the strongest impression. I heard in my heart the word, *"Sonship."*

I asked, "What are you saying to me? Father, what does sonship mean?"

The night had a myriad of night sounds. The lightning bugs were ablaze with a spectacle of lights. An owl was hooting. The campfire crackled with pops from gases in the wood. The setting was mystical. I then heard the words again softly spoken to my heart, *"You are My son. Be My son. Receive your sonship."*

I asked, "How do I receive my sonship?"

"Release your past. Abandon yourself to Me. Release your fears. Release control. Trust Me absolutely. Then you will embrace your sonship."

I realized that I was having a conversation with God and it just dawned on me. It was as if I could speak to Him and hear His reply as I would with another person. I had seen this happen with Gabe often. He had developed an ability to block out the rest of the world when he approached his Daddy, as he called Him. When that happened, it was just God and Gabe. Could I trust this communication with God, or was I only imagining that I could? Gabe assured me that if we seek God we will find Him, but we have to really seek Him. We have to block out all other voices and thoughts that come at us to hear Him. That is why getting away in a private setting such as I was in opens my heart's ears to God's voice. He also said that I needed to spend a lot of time in the Bible to learn what God values and dislikes to know that we hear His voice. He said that God's voice always speaks within the truth of scripture. I had been doing that, so I felt assured that what I was hearing was indeed God speaking to me and showing me the way to sonship.

I felt there was more for me to listen to if God was telling me my next steps in that direction. I cleaned up my dinner plate and got the camp neatened up. I was getting a little chilled with the night temperature dropping. So, a little hot water and a pouch of hot chocolate would be the perfect end to my meal and to get ready for my sleeping bag.

14 | An *Orphan* No More

I made my hot chocolate and leaned against the very boulder that I used two years before. It had been an amazing journey since that night. As I sipped the hot brew, I felt a peace fall over me that I cannot describe. I thought of the past few days. I thought of the skillful way Gabe had introduced me to the foundational pillars of God's character, as a means to assure me that He can be trusted. I thought about the bedrock of grace that every aspect of God's character and my relationship with Him is built on. I was assured that my relationship with Him is not, nor can it be, based on anything but God's grace to me. Gabe told me that this is a constant theme that runs from the beginning of my relationship with God through-out my life. He said I needed to establish this grace perspective as a bedrock, so that if I ever began to become performance-driven in my thinking to gain God's love, I can be steered back to a right perspective and be assured that I already have it and will never lose it.

I thought of that building beam Gabe showed me, and how it represents my faith. It is my faith that connects my life to all those wonderful attributes of God. He told me that my life would be built on these attributes as surely as a good house is built on a good foundation. But it would require my faith.

I thought about the field trip Gabe took me on where he showed me a comparison of the fields and the sheep of a good shepherd and a hireling. The difference that I saw was obvious. This visual lesson opened my eyes to Psalm 23 as never before, and I could embrace the thought of Christ being the Good Shepherd and me one of His sheep. The thoughts in Psalm 23, "He makes me lie down in green pastures, He leads me beside still waters, He restores my soul," became real to me as never before. Even now, around this campfire and on this weekend getaway to the mountains, I felt that my soul was being restored. Maybe this is what being restored means. It means to be restored to that which was lost and to have it returned. Jesus said that He came to seek and save that which was lost. What was lost? What was returned? I was lost. I was the prodigal son. I was an orphan of this world, longing for my adoption into God's family. Jesus came and sought after me. He found me. He saved me. He has restored to me the rights of sonship. Why would I deny myself anything that He has restored to me for any reason? Oh, what a foolish man I've been to not take all He offers to me.

My mind went back to the scripture Gabe and I discussed in Psalm 139. Key points jumped out to me confirming the completeness of my Good Shepherd's knowledge of me. One would have to have little imagination to not see the completeness of God's knowledge and intentionality of the use of His knowledge of me for my good. The foundation of grace that undergirds His knowledge assures me that this knowledge of me is for my good and welfare, and not to be an ever-present critical eye looking for every opportunity to find me in a wrong. Do I believe this theologically but fail to embrace it as truth and trust it? I think this might be the case for me.

God's care for me and those I love was so clearly and emotionally conveyed to me by a better picture of the intimate caring Shepherd who loves me. There can be no debate in the clearness of this point, if I believe scripture and the testimony of those who have been under that care. Do I believe this about Jesus theologically, but fail to embrace Him relationally? I think that this is also the case.

God's willingness to use all His assets and knowledge of me to bless me is also very clear in scripture. What I hadn't considered is how something I may do can hinder His ability to work on my behalf. What a revelation it was for me to realize that I could be my own worst enemy with having my prayers answered. Will I continue to get in the way of God's best plans for me because of willful sin, or a slothful, casual pursuit of Christ that keeps me from realizing the best He has to offer? I must not… any more. I must not!

How grateful I am for the underlying grace that empowers all of God's attributes to overcome my limitations and the separation that my sins could produce with me. His grace breaks through all those conditions. But do I adequately walk in His grace? When He tells me that His grace is sufficient for all my needs and for every challenge that I will ever face, do I even limit what He can do for me with His grace? The way I beat up on myself, and the way I stand afar from Him, even though He has invited me to leave my orphan spirit behind to embrace His sonship, tells me that I have a disconnect.

I am leaving so much grace that is offered to me on the table, simply because I think myself unworthy. Will I continue to do this?

My mentor Gabe spotted it clearly. Perhaps it is like he said. He had the same orphan spirit that kept him at a distance from God until he left it behind. This could make him spot that spirit clearly in me. The irony of this problem is I had never seen myself an orphan of the world, for I thought it would require being an orphan in a traditional sense. At first I didn't get it. But now I see that all people begin as orphans in a spiritual sense. We all must be adopted by Father God to come into His family. This is what happens when we trust in and receive Jesus. At that point we are given sonship. But some of us never lose the orphan identity and never embrace our sonship. It was now clear to me that this was my problem. This is why I would not enter in and stay in intimate fellowship with God. I held on to my old identity. The question now is, will I continue to hold on to it, or will I let go of it and grasp what God offers me?

After I finished my hot chocolate, I stood and walked around the little meadow I was in. It was now dark. My campfire lit the area around me with a soft glow reflecting off the boulders. Away from the fire and boulders, I looked toward the stream and into darkness beyond it. I was alone and would be unheard as I began my prayer. I offered my words loudly and sincerely. Tonight, the orphan must be asked to leave for God's son to emerge.

"Father, I never knew that an old perspective of myself that Gabe called the orphan spirit could be keeping me from coming closer to You. I can see that I have stood outside Your holy presence and been afraid to come close to You. Why have I done this?"

Spoken to my heart were these words, *"You have yet to abandon yourself to Me and trust Me absolutely. As a result, you hold on to a memory, a pain, and a shame that you will not release to Me. You hold on to an old image of yourself. This keeps you distant."*

"Why do I not release them to You, Lord? I want to!" I asked.

"Like so many of My other children, you think I would not love you if I truly knew you. That is why you need to real-ize that I know everything about you and love you still," the Lord answered. *"The orphan spirit will always hide from Me, and think itself unworthy to be loved by Me."*

"Lord why would You love me as You do? I can't understand it."

"That is the problem, dear child. You try to understand something you are incapable of understanding. You are also unwilling to accept anything that you do not understand. Unless you become as a little child with your trust in Me, and accept without fully understanding My ways, you will always hold on to the orphan spirit."

"How can I accept something that I don't understand? How can I believe something I don't see?" I said.

The Lord replied, *"It is called faith. With faith you do not have to understand or see something to believe it is true. But with faith you are given spiritual eyes to see that which cannot be seen otherwise. With faith you come to understand that which you were ignorant of before. Faith opens your heart and makes all things possible, for your faith is in Me."*

"Savior, it sounds like I must believe to see, to abandon to gain, and to release to be accepted. Everything seems so opposite of the ways of the world. Is it that these are the things that keep within me the orphan spirit?"

The Lord spoke clearly, *"Yes. You must believe to receive, and release that you may gain."*

After the Lord spoke these things to my heart, I continued to pace my little area around the campfire. A flood of thoughts that Gabe had given to me came to mind. My thoughts about God's characteristics and the unique way He loves washed over me. The inner guardedness that I had grown up with began to loosen, and a hidden tension was being released. It was as if a rubber band that had been wound extra tight for years was being slowly un-wound. I felt I was finally letting go of an old image of myself and accepting the image God wanted me to have. In my new perspective I literally saw myself stepping into a room with the banquet table Gabe described, dressed in new clothes. The old clothes of my orphan spirit were removed and replaced with those fit for a son. At the head of the table was my Heavenly Daddy and around the table were adopted children, likewise in new clothes. I knew that God was confirming that indeed I am His son, and I had finally come home.

During this surreal period of prayer, I lost awareness of the time. I had been so engrossed with my interaction with God that I hadn't realized that my fire was now down to a few burning coals. I had no doubt been to a place I'd never been before in my interaction with God. If I had any doubts about God's presence and His complete acceptance of me before, it was now gone from me. I was no longer an orphan. I was a son.

15 | *Walking* in Sonship

It wasn't long after my extensive interaction with the
Lord that I threw a couple of logs on the fire to keep
it going, and then went to my tent for a much-needed
night's sleep. When I snuggled into my sleeping bag
I felt for the first time a security unlike anything I had
ever experienced before. Now I knew that I was not
alone or unprotected, and I was now convinced that
what I felt before was the orphan spirit in me. Gone was
the need to calculate or strategize solutions while I laid
in bed until I fell asleep just to feel safe and guarded.
Found was a peace that God had it all in His hands and
I could trust Him … a real, burden-lifting trust in Him
to show me the way to navigate life. I felt that I could
now lay my head down on my pillow and rest under the
sovereign authority of God. Sovereignty is just that. It
means He is over all, and all things must come through

Him before it comes to His kids, and I am one of His kids. I am His son, and He is my Daddy. I had finally understood what I was missing and what Gabe said I needed. I needed to be loved by the best Daddy a man would ever have, and to have Him affirm me as His son. Then the orphan spirit is released.

In a sleepy, but relaxed voice, I prayed out loud a heartfelt prayer. These simple words came from what I was feeling deep within. I prayed, "Goodnight, Daddy. I look forward to seeing You tomorrow. I love You." I then fell into a deep sleep, feeling wrapped in His love as never before.

The next day I woke later in the morning than normal. I made a cup of coffee and spent time reading my Bible and journaling about my breakthrough the night before. Words were flowing from me like rivers of water. I had much to say, and quickly wrote every thought down as it came into my mind. After several hours I realized I hadn't eaten breakfast and I was hungry. I decided to break camp and pick up a hamburger at the little café next to the general store. I planned to go by Gabe's house on the way home, for I had some big news to tell him.

 I arrived later at Gabe's house and he was sitting on
his front porch. I left my truck and started walking
toward him. The closer I got to him, the bigger the smile
showed on his face. When I got to the steps of the porch
he said, "You don't have to tell me one thing. Your face
says it all. The orphan is no more, and a son of God is at
my steps today. Am I right?"

He was right. I had no idea how he could have seen it
in me. But it was true. I was a different man than had
left him the day before. I felt loved, and I felt an internal
strength and peace that had made its way to my demean-
or. I guess that kind of thing really shows.

On another return trip to see Gabe in the near future, he
would help me understand another critical association
with Father God that would help me maintain a deeper
and more sustainable connection with Him. I repeat: It
would become the most critical step in my journey with
Christ. However, like Gabe's skilled unfolding of the
need for a good foundation, this trip built the foundation
for the next critical step I reference. This present foundation required that I fully embrace my sonship with the
Father, and then He would show me what was next.

I have come to see that authentic discipleship is a con-

tinuous unfolding of getting to know God better, and
the removal of those hindrances that stand in the way.
I'm on a journey … a spiritual journey with getting to
know Him. I know it will take an eternity to fully know
Him, for He is unfathomable to the human mind. What
I know about Him causes me to worship Him. But there
is so much more to discover. This trip has made me love
Him more than ever before, because I have discovered
His love for me. All followers of Christ are on their own
journey. Though it may look different for each individual,
the destination is the same. It is to be led into an increas-
ing depth with close proximity to Jesus Christ, and our
love for Him. Each step is strategically orchestrated by
the Holy Spirit to show us how to get there. However,
we can go no further in our journey until each step is
made through complete surrender and trust. If we do
not choose to surrender those aspects of our life that He
reveals and that stand in the way of our journey, we can
become stagnated in a frustrating, fruitless life. So many
men and women have found this to be true in their own
life. They ask, "why?" It is clear it is because they will
not surrender the things that get in the way.

The surrender of my orphan spirit to embrace my
sonship would now allow me to move beyond it. Had
I not surrendered it and taken what was offered to me,

I would have seen myself as an orphan and would live like an orphan for the rest of my life, even though God had made me His son and wanted me to embrace it. God wants more for His children than the stagnation we settle for, and we have to take from Him what He offers, and on His terms.

After I shared with Gabe the joy of my recognized sonship and the surrender of the orphan spirit he told me, "That is a critical hurdle, for you are now able to be led into a life that He wants for you. Your journey with Him will now grow more quickly and deeply than you have ever known."

"What do I do next, Gabe?" I asked, ready to step into my journey more enthusiastically.

"The first thing I want you to do is bring your sweet wife to see me. Let's not forget her and the importance of her spiritual journey. After all, she is God's gift to you and she needs be nurtured along in her identity as God's daughter. You also need to spend time with your Heavenly Daddy and get to know Him through the new perspective that you now have. Continue to embrace your sonship. Later when it is right, I will show you your next steps."

This exhortation resonated in my heart, so I set up a time for Dottie and me to come back for a visit with Gabe. Many of my future visits with Gabe would include her, for she grew to love him as much as me. Like me, she would benefit from his wise council.

I told my wise mentor goodbye for the time being. I drove home with joy to share with Dottie what had happened. Though there were many points concerning the reasons to trust God that were made—His grace, His knowledge of me, His nurturing care of me, His willingness to be involved, and His ability to help me—the one point that invited me to trust Him the most is that I am no longer an orphan of the world. I am now a son of God. He is my Daddy. It is this perspective that causes me to love Him and trust Him as never before. It is now the strongest part of my foundation. I hope you will find this for your life as well.